DEDICATION

To my brother Adam and best friend Hayley, for journeying with me to create some of these wonderful memories. I miss you and can't wait for the day to come where we can share the karaoke stage again! To my friend Emma who helped me redo the title as the first one clearly wasn't going to work! Last but not least, to my mum and dad, Annette and David (I, of course, miss you too!) - thank you for believing in me and for all the love and support you have given me. xxx

GW00391160

THE TWISTS AND TURNS OF A TRAVELLER

LIFE LESSONS, ADVENTURES AND EVERYTHING IN BETWEEN

TESSA SILLIFANT

TABLE OF CONTENTS

CHAPTER 1:
HOW IT ALL BEGAN

Growing up, I had more than my fair share of challenges. In primary school, I lost family members and a friend, and somehow upset my teachers by just being me! Throughout secondary school, I wore braces, had severe acne and was bullied by my peers. I had numerous bouts of tonsillitis and had to sit for many exams with a fever and inflamed tonsils. Academically, I scraped by with enough grades to get me into college, but when I was ready to break out into the 'real world', potential employers told me I was unemployable.

Looking back, I had very little awareness of my resilience and perseverance and where these would take me in life. I just knew that I needed money to live and that I needed to fulfil my dreams to take me to where I needed to be.

FINDING WORK

I spent most of my childhood on a farm in Cornwall, the South West of England, and although this was a beautiful part of the country, opportunities were hard to come by. Most people entered a job between 16-18 years of age and would remain there until they retired. I didn't like that idea, but I knew I had to start earning before I could ever be in charge of making a decision like that.

After going through the Yellow Pages (a large book of business contacts) to write and introduce myself to all the local businesses, and repeatedly visiting the local job centre for daily updates, I was invited to participate in a number of cringe-worthy interviews and eventually, I got lucky and was offered my first full-time job.

THE BIG WIDE WORLD

The feeling of being lucky sadly wore off quickly and I soon found myself bored, not feeling "needed" at work. I didn't have enough work to keep me busy throughout the day and I was unsure how I could contribute to the organisation, what my purpose was and the direction I was headed.

I did the only thing I knew how to do at that age with a large monthly paycheck and minimum bills to spend my money on; I lived a socially enriched existence and suffered silently with raging hangovers!

No matter what people say, partying hard takes its toll on everyone and after a few months of my "play hard" lifestyle, I found that I was questioning my existence and thinking that there had to be more to life than sleeping through entire weekends and having no memory of the previous day. I knew it was time to get myself out of the temptations of boredom, so I decided it was time to save money and move out. With this idea, I diligently saved so that I could buy furniture as something physical to show for my money.

CRUNCH TIME

On a particularly dull day at work, after working there for nearly a year, my boss called me into his office to give me a verbal warning for wearing my suit jacket sleeves rolled up. I left his office in shock and the next day, I returned with my written notice and left shortly after to embark on a three and a half week holiday that had already been planned months before!

Coming back, I knew I had to work hard to find another job as getting a job locally wasn't looking easy. However, because I had been saving for a while, I had enough money for a deposit to rent a flat, I had furniture and a little bit of experience behind me to be able to start afresh somewhere else. I did exactly that and reinvented myself in one of the 'big' cities close by; the neighbouring county of Devon!

SURVIVAL MODE

Moving out completely changed me. I had no idea that rent wasn't the only thing I needed to factor in when working out a salary to realistically survive on! I needed to pay Council Tax, a TV license and keep up with my car bills. I needed to pay for electricity, water, and a phone line! I decided to go without a TV and a phone line, but kept the car as security for getting home to family if and when needed which eventually proved to be pointless because as each month went by, I never had any money left for petrol! However, it wasn't long before I was scouring the streets for any lost coins and would save the treasures to fuel my electric meter and laundry costs! I'd live off of 18 pence spaghetti and 15 pence bread and would use 10 pence in a payphone to call family and ask them to call me back. I would stay late at work as the office was always warm and on those cold winter nights, I would use the heat from my hair dryer to warm my bed before jumping in! I walked everywhere, rain or shine, and when Christmas came, I took on a second job to pay for presents and petrol to get home!

TURNING POINT

After about three years of living my early twenties on the verge of poverty, I felt old before my time. I was tired of barely surviving each day and continuously having to decline social events. I took a long look at my life and asked myself what had happened to all of my dreams. Surely, this wasn't the norm for every young lady in her twenties trying to make it on her own.

Living in a time before the internet was widely accessible, I went to the local library and browsed the shelves for some inspiration and soon came across the travel section. Flicking through the pages, I saw sights that looked incredible but felt so out of reach. I went home disheartened and sat on my bed frustrated. Australia popped into my mind with the koala bears, kangaroos, Sydney Opera House, Bondi beach and the sunlight. Why can't I go there? Why not? The questions came out differently, but the answers remained the same. I just didn't have the money. I tore at myself, my mind getting louder. WHY CAN'T I GO THERE? WHY NOT? Surely, there was another reason; it couldn't just be money? When I reflected on it for a while, indeed money was the only reason I could not go.

Not being one to give up easily, I decided that if it was money I needed, then I was going to get it and as a result of that decision, I took on four jobs and worked 80 hours a week. By day, I worked as a legal secretary, at night, I stacked shelves. Over the weekends, I worked in retail as a counter assistant, and on the odd Wednesday, I babysat my neighbour's friend's children.

Little did I know the decision I made that day would leave me worn out and bed ridden with exhaustion and glandular fever for several weeks; only a couple of months before I was to embark on my adventure of a lifetime! However, I got better and made it onto the plane (despite several hiccups along the way to the airport - more on that later) and I can honestly say, hand on heart, I've never looked back. The decision I made that day, together with the experiences and adventures that came as a result of the hard work I put in to make my dreams a reality, taught me so many valuable life lessons that have stayed close to me ever since. As a result of my experiences and the choices I have made, I am resilient, I have a high level of perseverance and I have an inner strength that I don't think I would have attained without enduring the difficult times and challenges that life threw to me. I've learnt that it's not always the destination that brings you the warm feeling; it's the effort you've made to get there that makes all the difference.

So after spending years comparing myself to others and wondering why I'm slightly different or why I chose to take the path less trodden and opt out of the 'easy' way, I decided it was time to embrace the experiences (good and bad) that I have been blessed with, keep those memories alive and share a part of my story. I understand that travelling isn't for everyone, however, you can choose to create memories and experiences for yourself that can enrich your life, inspire you, teach you and motivate you to be the best version of yourself. Those experiences also have the potential to change and impact your life for the better.

The Journey Uncovered

So this book provides a realistic insight into the good, the bad and the damn right ugly for anyone thinking about travelling. This book is for those who are connected closely with someone who is about to embark on an adventure, to enable them to understand some of the challenges they may face while they are away from family, friends and loved ones. This book is also for those who have experienced sadness and challenges and want an insight from someone who has come through to the other side and embraced and conquered fears, challenges and pain.

Regardless of your background, status, character or culture, everyone has the right to dream big, and everyone should have the right to work towards making their dreams a reality. So whether you decide to travel or not, this is completely your choice, but promise me that you will laugh always and enjoy the good things that life has to offer you, because you owe it to yourself to make good choices and to be happy. Love and be loved, and be the best version of yourself because you only get one chance at life.

So what are you waiting for? Are you coming along for the ride?

Welcome to my journey!
xx

CHAPTER 2:
ADVENTURE, ADVENTURE, ADVENTURE - NEW EXPERIENCES TO IGNITE YOUR SENSES

I am the kind of girl that likes experiences that allow my senses to come alive. For me, this means taking in new sights, smells, tastes and traditions! The more I see, the more I crave; the more I learn, the more I want to explore; and the more I meet new people, the more I want to hear about their stories which opens up the curiosity to visit and immerse myself in other cultures of the world. These experiences present a wealth of opportunity and do a lot for your personal development as you often find yourself out of your comfort zone, solving problems and strengthening your resilience as you navigate the unknown. Taking on unexpected challenges, overcoming fears and learning to live with yourself and your thoughts (that some people spend years fighting or hiding from) are also experiences that you may have! Of course, there is also the added bonus of having fun along the way and developing a new sense of appreciation for the natural beauty of the world. There is a priceless sense of personal satisfaction, accomplishment and excitement to be fortunate enough to experience these things.

FIRST EXPERIENCES

I remember my first adventure like it was yesterday. It was my 'test run' to Wales in my late teens which tested my ability to see if I could 'survive' exploring a place I didn't know alone. I knew it wasn't very far away, but I saw it as a challenge to see how I would find the whole experience.

Although I travelled alone, my trip included a mix of exploring and catching up with friends who were away studying. I caught trains and buses and stayed in local Bed and Breakfasts. I went to Bristol, Cardiff, Pembroke, Haverford West and St David's! It was such an adventure! I remember sitting on the sand at a beautiful beach one day, as the wind blew through my hair, while I read a book, feeling so proud of myself! I had actually done what I had set out to do! There were moments that I knew I needed to get stronger at but I had done it! I was in a country that spoke two languages, living off the budget I had set out for myself, visiting the places I had mapped out before I left, learning a little bit more about myself every day and I was getting better at problem solving.

CHALLENGES

One of the areas I knew I had to improve on was being able to comfortably eat alone at a table! I remember staying in one of the Bed and Breakfast places and pacing up and down my room trying to psych myself up to go downstairs for breakfast! I hadn't fully realized that something so simple could bring me so much angst. I remember being so overwhelmed by my thoughts that there was a moment where I felt physically stuck in my room.

Thankfully, after hating on myself for a while and pacing up and down my room, I was able to calm my mind and rationalize the situation. I knew I had to find a way to feel confident enough to go downstairs to the breakfast room and eat on my own. I asked myself how I could get out of this state of mind and after scouring the room, I noticed a radio on the bedside table. I turned it on and soon found a positive upbeat song that got my hips swaying and lifted my mood so much that a surge of inner confidence rushed through me. I knew I had to act on this feeling fast so I grabbed my wallet and my room key and just walked straight to the breakfast room with my head held high. I just did it!

However, eating in the breakfast room was as awful as I had expected! I was seated at a table, on my own, in the middle of the room and I felt everyone's eyes fixated on me while I nervously sat there fidgeting and waiting for my food to arrive. I don't know whether my perception was accurate or whether my vivid imagination ran wild that morning, but I remember feeling as though every woman in the room was looking at me like I was some sort of home wrecker and that I was there to steal their husband! I realize now that this was quite an irrational thought to have had, but at the time, I felt their eyes pierce through me with instant hatred!

Once my food arrived, I ate at high speed and then vanished back up to my room to pack. I remember taking a few deep breaths and analyzing what had just happened. Yes, I had successfully completed the task at hand, but I felt exhausted from all the nervous energy I had put upon myself. How can I make tomorrow's breakfast less stressful? As this was before the days where our phones could provide us with all the entertainment we needed, I decided to take a book with me next time so that I didn't have to look around the room and let my thoughts get the better of me. So the next day, in a different place, I did exactly that and had a completely different experience. Result; Fear number one conquered!

REFLECTION

Since that trip to Wales, I have been to a number of different places around the world and have experienced many wonderful things! From the night markets in Thailand to seeing the pandas in China, and walking along a secluded part of the Great Wall, to volunteering in Sweden in a Computer Trainee Centre. I have also volunteered in an orphanage in Eastern Europe and seen the pyramids in Egypt. I've danced all night in Cyprus and have achieved my dreams of walking along Bondi beach, seeing a show at Sydney's Opera House and seeing the koala bears and kangaroos in Australia!

I have slept in a beach fale in Samoa and have gone sand boarding on the sand dunes in Fiji! I have ridden in overnight trains, scooters, rickshaws, canoes, water taxis, ferries, gondola's, trams and tuk-tuks! I have been involved in a stunt drive, climbed mountains, skydived over lakes, paraglided over beaches, driven a tank and heli-hiked through glaciers!

There are so many amazing and beautiful things that this world has to offer us and travelling is definitely a hobby that never grows old! If any of these experiences I've mentioned light a fire within and inspire you to knock off some of your own 'bucket list' items, I dare you to find a way to explore your inner traveller and go and see what the world has to offer you because life is exactly what you make it and it can be filled with action, adventure and adrenalin if you wish it to be!

CHAPTER 3:
JOURNEY TO SELF DISCOVERY

Before I set off on my adventure to Australia, I remember thinking how restricted I had been at my office job to maintain a particular style while having this strong feeling within to be different! There were rules on the clothes you wore, any piercings and tattoos had to be covered up and jewelry had to be at a minimum. So of course, when I made the decision to travel, there seemed to be no better time to reinvent myself than just before embarking on a journey to the other side of the world!

Once the idea was in my mind, it became etched so deeply that I just needed to break free! So off came my long blond hair which was cut into a sort of pixie style, out came the hair dye which was a brown-red tint, and off I went to the local tattoo and piercing shop to get my eyebrow pierced! I am not going to lie, the piercing was really painful and my body quickly rejected the metal object that it only lasted a couple of weeks. The scar however still remains and I'll never forget the sense of excitement I felt that day; the feeling of being free to make decisions I had otherwise felt restricted from making.

Travelling with short cropped hair was really easy to manage as I moved around from hostel to hostel. I didn't have to worry about waking other people in the dorm room with my noisy hairdryer and I didn't need to spend ages using it to dry my hair. However, dying it a dark colour when I was naturally blond was a little more tricky to maintain while on the go all the time. Believe me when I say that dying your hair in hostel toilets can be very hard to manage and can get extremely messy when you're confined to a small space and are conscious of splattering hair dye on the walls or staining the decor! I also found that whenever I was exploring warmer parts of the world, my hair was exposed to the sun a lot more, making the hair dye last for shorter as the sun's rays naturally lightened my hair and sometimes, turned it orange! So finding the time, energy and money to frequently dye my hair added another layer to the challenge which I certainly hadn't anticipated from the start.

MORAL OF THE STORY

This experience was one where I looked back and laughed and thought, "you know what, I'm glad I tried it!" At the time, it enabled me to recreate myself and have the courage to be the person I wanted to be, which was what I desperately needed. What better way to do this than when you are around strangers who don't know any different! It helped me to start afresh with no questions asked. I was able to take control, make adjustments, trial them and embrace them! It was empowering to be so carefree and have the space and freedom to find myself!

CONQUERING FEARS

Looking back, my travel days were the days I learnt the most about myself, the world and people. There were many good times where people looked out for each other and showed care and concern for you and your wellbeing. There were many moments of encouragement and camaraderie, especially in frightening situations!

I remember when I was in Fiji. I joined the Fiji Experience bus and on that trip, I had to jump out of a waterfall to get to the other side to continue the tour. I had done a sky dive and a paraglide so having a fear of heights had never crossed my mind, yet I stood on the edge frozen, watching the water pour in front of me. My palms sweaty and my heart racing, I had a strong feeling that I may not be able to bring myself to jump.

Not being a strong swimmer and knowing how fierce the water can be, my fear was real. Yet the memory of going down a waterslide in Spain and seeing my bikini top floating away from me also filled my mind and contributed to my reluctance to jump.

One by one, members of the tour ran and jumped off the edge to immerse themselves in tropical waters. I, on the other hand, stood rigidly, looking for another way down!

It wasn't long before all the other members of the tour were waiting for me, chanting my name, giving me words of encouragement. Three, two, one, I ran, I jumped and I got taken by the current and a rescue boat had to come and save me! Oh the shame! But thankfully, my swim wear was in one piece!

MORAL OF THE STORY

History does not always repeat itself (and thank goodness for one-piece swim wear!) Tours are usually really well organized and have carefully laid out back-up plans for situations and eventualities. So have faith, it will be okay and be proud of the giant leap you took that day because you challenged yourself and that takes courage!

LIFE SKILLS AND LOOKING AFTER YOURSELF

Life is a never ending journey of experiences to learn from and enrich your life. Some experiences are positive and will bring you joy, reward, satisfaction, love and excitement while others bring you sadness, loss and suffering. If you experience the sad times while travelling, they can be particularly hard because sometimes, you need more than words to help you through it. You may want hugs, company, compassion and someone who just gets you, someone you don't have to explain your situation to, someone who just knows you enough to know what you need.

There is no controlling the sad times, they can happen at any time and in any manner. It could be an event, a circumstance, a memory that triggers the distance between you and your loved ones or an intense feeling of homesickness that just overwhelms and washes over you like a tidal wave.

While you are away travelling, it is really important to reach out to others, speak with family and friends about how you are feeling and allow yourself to feel the emotions you are carrying. Sometimes, I find it hard to process what I'm feeling, or why I'm feeling the way I am, so I write in a journal. Usually, the words tend to flow out on paper almost as a form of release as they sort themselves into a story while I write. I also practice gratitude by thinking about all the reasons I am lucky and grateful. These range from the moments I have had with people, to the ability to appreciate the natural beauty around me during walks in the parks and the amazing people I have had in my life, to the food that I can eat and the things I learnt that day.

Travelling can be hard because you meet and connect with people through the experiences you share in that moment.

Depending on the situation, these connections may just be at the surface level where they are unlikely to ever amount to what you have had with your best friend since high school. In these situations they become people you share the present moment with.

Being outside of your comfort zone while travelling can reveal a number of insecurities and challenges which can also bring out the humane parts of others as people want to help you or share their experiences and support you. It can also be in those raw, vulnerable and unexpected moments where you connect deeply with others. That is one of the magical parts of travelling as you learn, share and engage with others who may start out as strangers but later, potentially become life-long friends.

Navigating the unknown, experiencing new things, meeting people of different backgrounds, experiences and cultures certainly opens up your eyes to a world bigger than you have ever known. It is in these moments that deep, rich learning about life really occurs. You gain a number of valuable life skills through travelling. From budgeting to problem solving, communicating and the ability to find your way in unfamiliar environments; travelling sharpens and develops skills. There are many opportunities to learn about yourself so that you can understand how you handle certain situations and where your strengths are. There will be times when you have to think on your feet, act fast and make decisions based on instinct and there will also be times when you learn your lessons the hard way.

Learning the Hard Way

I remember once when I went to buy a flower from a florist on a beach in Spain. I do not know why I did this, because I am not one for buying flowers. But I remember she called out asking for "one English penny" and I felt drawn by the connection to England. As she called, I made my way towards her and when I was near, she took my wallet from my grip and magically slid all the notes out without me knowing! It was only when I got back to the place I was staying at, that I realized what had happened and sadly, that was the only money I had for that entire trip! Thankfully, I was away with my best friend and we had already anticipated the trip being a cost intensive one and had purchased food from the local supermarket to keep the costs at a minimum. However, it meant that for the remainder of the trip, we had to be frugal and make things last and I was extremely lucky to have been able to rely on my best friend sharing her hard earned money with me. This experience taught me to learn how to find enjoyment from the simple things in life. From enjoying the free things nature provides us, like parks and beaches, to finding things to smile and laugh about because things can only get better, right?

Moral of the Story

There are many elements in life that are beyond your control, so it is important to put yourself in the safest situation possible. In some situations, you may have a gut feeling that something is not quite right. You may not know or understand why, but it is important to listen to it.

This particular incident happened in the middle of the day, right in front of me! While it was orchestrated as a result of my own naivety, there may be situations that you have less control over. So when you go out, try and think ahead and have your safety at the back of your mind. Think about how you are going to get home, the people around you, your frame of mind, the frame of mind of others, where your money is, whether you can store your money in different places (e.g. different wallets, locked away in your backpack or a money belt etc.), the influence others have on you and whether the situation sounds too good to be true, because chances are, it might just be!

CHAPTER 4:
MONEY, MONEY, GLORIOUS MONEY

Nowadays, there are many more opportunities and ways to do things on a budget. There are options like couch surfing where you can stay at someone's house for free and mix with the locals and travel to different locations at a minimal cost. There are volunteering opportunities where accommodation and food can be provided during your stay and incorporated into the costs of your experience. There are also endless tour and accommodation options that cater to many different budget ranges.

Going on holiday or travelling can be really expensive. You want to experience as much as you can, you want to have incredible memories of each place and you want it to be special. However, there are ways you can make it cheap.

VENICE

I remember on one of my trips with my best friend, we decided that we needed to make it a low-cost budget trip even before we got on the plane. We were heading to Venice for five days and wondered how easy this would be, so we decided to challenge ourselves to spend no more than 100 Euros for the entire duration. We had paid for our accommodation and breakfast was included, so we felt it was do-able and it totally was!

Arriving at Venice, we hopped on a bus to take us into the centre of Venice and we soon realized that the bus only accepted a bus card which neither of us had. The driver took one look at our suitcases and smiled and said, "take a seat." We sat down and giggled to each other because we had already unexpectedly received a nice gesture from a local to help us with our challenge of spending as little as possible.

Getting off the bus, we decided to walk to our accommodation and soon discovered that there were many bridges with steps that we needed to pull our suitcases up over. We then realized that maybe, just maybe, the bus driver was already fully aware of what we had to navigate!

One by one, we struggled through each step and started to regret packing so much for such a short trip, but navigating the narrow roads and taking in the sights of Venice was a beautiful experience!

During our trip, we decided to make the challenge fun for ourselves, so we recorded a video diary a few times each day, capturing all the things that we came across and were excited to explore. We walked everywhere, utilized the complimentary breakfast and saved some of those goodies for lunch and shopped at the local supermarket for dinner options. We explored every part of Venice by foot and no matter how easy we thought it would be to get lost within the labyrinth of narrow streets and picturesque bridges and houses, we always found our way to where we wanted to be. We tasted gelato and spent time in cafes for a hot chocolate and enjoyed the local way of transport that was just like a gondola but at a fraction of the cost.

I also got sick on that trip and came down with a head cold and a chesty cough, so I decided to sacrifice some of my spending money on some medicine to recover quicker than I probably would have if I just soldiered on. Surprisingly, I was also able to buy myself a necklace from one of the market stalls and arrived at the airport in Venice with seven Euros left for a snack as well as lots of fun memories with my friend!

MORAL OF THE STORY

Going away doesn't have to be expensive, you can have fun and have lots of memories on a budget. You may need to plan and organize in advance, you may need to sacrifice some "luxuries", but often, it is the adventure and story you set for yourself in your head that makes it memorable and meaningful. All the years later, my friend and I still reminisce over that adventurous holiday and we always maintain that any place is nice to be, as long as you have good company!

CHAPTER 5:
BITTER SWEET

While I was travelling, I learnt that some of my best moments could quickly turn into the worst and when you are miles away from home, these can be really difficult to deal with.

When I was temping, I was invited to a karaoke event that my company had organized to take place in the office. Within me, my heart did a little jump and a skip because I love to sing and it brought back lots of wonderful memories of me back home with my best friend belting out Whitney Houston hits on a Friday night! On the outside, I was a little nervous because I am an awkward person who takes a while to warm up to people. My colleagues hadn't really seen the inner me and I wasn't sure if I was ready for them to! I was quite pumped because I had been saving hard for the next trip and had neglected my inner need to belt out a tune and swing my hips hard, so I decided to consciously make the effort to let my hair down and worry about the consequences next week!

I do not really drink wine, so I did not need much to loosen me up. I think a couple of sips did the trick! There were a few microphones so we teamed up to find songs and sang in pairs. There was this lovely lady who I had talked to earlier that day about my love for Whitney and she secretly went and put our names down for that tune. When the song came on, I felt every ounce of me come alive, she passed me the microphone and we sang together and I was completely in the zone! There were a few high bits that I could not bring myself to try, so I mimed those and included a little dance instead. I think I must have been so much in the zone that I had forgotten everyone was in the room watching me. I looked over to the lady I was supposed to be singing with and realized she was sitting down on a chair opposite me looking as though she had stopped singing a long time ago!

The song finished and there was this deadly silence. I took the microphone away from my mouth and froze. My mind racing, I could not quite figure out what had just happened. I must have closed my eyes when I was singing. Did something happen that I missed?

Before my mind could race anymore, everyone began to jump up and down, cheering and rushing over to me, hugging and praising me like I was some sort of celebrity! I was blown away by their reaction. The guy managing the sound came up to me afterwards and said he used to be a singer in a band and that I had what it took to be a singer as well, I just needed to learn how to breathe properly when I sing long notes and to train my voice for those high notes. I stood there, jaw wide open in shock. He went on to say I had amazing stage presence and that I blew everyone away with my ability to capture the audience.

Um, errr, me? Are you sure? Everyone joined in singing my praises. I felt like I was on cloud nine. I replayed his words in my head over and over again! My whole being was smiling! He said I had what it took to be a singer, something I had admired in others my whole life.

On my way home that night, I stopped by the payphone to call the UK with my cheap calling card (oh how times have changed!). I could not get hold of anyone to share my news which I so desperately wanted to share, so I headed to the internet cafe to send a bulk email to everyone I could think of, to relay each and every moment of the amazing evening I had just had!

At the cafe, I opened my emails and one stood out to me and I knew I needed to read it. It had the name of a friend from back home in the subject heading, but it was not from her. I opened it and I was told that my friend had been battling cancer and the cancer had spread throughout her body. I kept reading the email trying to tell myself that I was misinterpreting the message, that what I was reading was not real. But it was and reality came crashing down. Yes, I had had an amazing night, but another person's story was very different. Overrun with emotion, I did not really know what to do. I paid up my internet fee, went home and cried myself to sleep because sadly, life brings with it many twists and turns.

MORAL OF THE STORY

Many things in this world are beyond our control. We do not know the next time we may see someone, or if we have already seen them for the last time. We do not know other people's circumstances or situation. When you are travelling and are on a high from all the new experiences you have had, it is easy to get caught up in your own world. Sometimes, people do not want to burst your bubble and do not want to worry or upset you, so you may not always be told as things unfold or happen. This is an extremely hard reality because it reminds you so deeply of the distance between you and how precious life is. But at the same time, we have to live our lives. Our own time can be snatched away from us out of the blue, so we owe it to ourselves to make sure we are also doing things that make us happy.

I do not know if being so far away is a blessing or a curse. On one hand, I am so far away from family and friends, it is hard. The pain is raw and real but you have to find a way to manage that. The distance has been too far and it is too expensive to go home for every occasion, happy or sad.

I watch friends travel on a different life path via Facebook. I see them get married and have families. I have learnt that life does not stand still for you. People change, places change, feelings associated with activities change.

You can be so far removed from friends and family that the distance can be really hard, yet the memories of experiences shared can remain and I hold those dear to my heart and count my blessings for all the good times that I have shared with others because those times have enriched my life and have taught me that no matter where you are in the world or in your life, people are important and people matter and it is the people in your life that impact you and make you the person you become.

While times can be incredibly hard, I try and appreciate the good times and embrace them wholeheartedly because love, happiness and kindness make the world go round and are the things that people are remembered for. Live in the moment and appreciate what is in front of you, as you really do not know how long people will be in your life and those times may be something that you will look back at and see with a different lens and always cherish.

CHAPTER 6:
CULTURAL DIFFERENCES

One thing I quickly learnt while travelling was that no matter what you want to do or where you want to go, you will always come across people. If you can understand, respect, tolerate, interpret and appreciate others, you will put yourself in a better position to handle an array of situations that you may find yourself in due to differences in culture. Whether it is because you are on the go all the time, exploring different places, joining tours, meeting people in hostels or through volunteering opportunities. Or perhaps, you have a work visa and you are settling in a place for a few months to earn some extra money to help fund the next part of your adventure, in which case, you will be meeting new people at work, finding a temporary place to live and living life like the locals do!

When you set yourself up to work in a different country, you can find yourself earning in a foreign currency, abiding by different rules and coming across noticeable changes in etiquette, language, culture and world views. You may need to set up a bank account in the country you are in, or you may need to think about what skills you have that are relevant to the work that is available in that particular area. You may need to brush up your language skills or be open to learning new skills as you try your luck at something completely different, just because you can!

Working in a different country will guarantee the need to navigate, acclimatize, and maintain a number of cultural differences as you enter into a world that is new to you and wade through unchartered waters.

LEARNING THE LINGO!

When I first arrived and began work in New Zealand, everything was different, yet remarkably the same. While I had lived in a city previously, I had not worked in a high rise building that looked out across a waterfront and city. As you can imagine, the view was spectacular but the downfall came when a fire drill put the lifts out of action and hordes of staff had to navigate their way down the long, narrow and windy flights of stairs that stiffened your calf muscles for days after. The climate in New Zealand was similar but at the opposite end of what I was used to. Christmas was shared with summer sunshine, barbeques, the beach and images of Santa in a t-shirt and my June birthday was now to be celebrated in winter.

When I secured my first temp job, I quickly realized that there were also many subtle differences in the workplace that would keep me on my toes to try and decipher what was going on around me.

This became apparent on my first day as a receptionist when I was greeted by a co-worker who uttered the words "can you pass me the "twink?" Now, for someone who does not like to admit they do not know something, I can tell you that this was an anxiety-inducing moment, particularly for my first encounter with someone I did not know, in an organisation I was not familiar with. Thoughts raced through my mind. Who is this person? What will their response to me be?

However, I had no reason to be afraid as most people in this world enjoy helping other people and there is no shame in speaking up and asking, "what do you mean?" So with that, I could soon add "twink" to my repertoire of kiwi (New Zealand) slang and learnt that it is the wonderful, magical correcting fluid the British often refer to by its brand name, *Tip-ex.*

On my second day in the workplace, the CEO introduced himself to me wearing board shorts and thongs and offered me a bowl of pineapple lumps and chocolate fish! Now, before you start imagining the thongs, they are what the British call "flip flops" and are worn on your feet during summer and go quite well with the board shorts! However, as you can imagine, this is not quite the average image you have of the CEO of a large organisation. Nevertheless, I was grateful for the unique welcome and offer of pineapple lumps and chocolate fish which were a nice way to enjoy some of New Zealand's iconic kiwiana sweet treats!

Having had the experience of being in top-down hierarchical organaisations in the UK, I soon came to realise that life in New Zealand was quite different! While we shared the same English language, I often found myself stumped by a few curveball phrases that often left me slightly confused.

"I'm heading to the dairy, would you like anything?" and "Don't forget to pack your togs" became phrases that I had to quickly get used to!

A dairy, as I found out, was not a place to milk the cows but a place you could buy milk or a newspaper or even perhaps a chocolate fish. Of course, togs were what you wore for the beach when you wanted to go into the sea!

I have to admit, one of my most cringe-worthy moments was when I went to the Dr's to have a medical examination and was asked to remove my pants. Thankfully, I had the confidence to speak up and question the Dr. and realised that New Zealand share the American meaning of pants as trousers and not under garments or knickers as I knew. Phew!

STAYING OUT OF TROUBLE!

Throughout my traveller days, there were times when I found myself trying to stay out of trouble due to cultural differences or plain misunderstandings! I often laugh and flinch at my first night staying at a backpacker hostel. I was travelling on my own and wanted to make some traveller friends, so I was really happy when I checked into the hostel and received a free drink voucher for the bar next door. In the evening, I went there and offered my voucher to a group of lively souls as a way to make connections. While we introduced ourselves and shared travel stories, I later found myself in the situation of talking my way out of doing the zero-ball game-of-pool, walk-of-shame challenge. The Scots I had innocently introduced myself to were keen on playing some pool and I thought I was quite good so when they offered me to play with them, I happily agreed. However, they apparently played by the rules of walking around the pool table naked if you missed potting the ball. Of course, they only announced this rule to me after they realised how poor my game skills were and this may have been a drunken plot made against me in the moment or a general test of my humour! While my drinking culture etiquette was tested along with my ability to think quickly, I did manage to win them round with organising a round of shots instead. *Double phew!*

HOME SWEET HOME

While I have always appreciated that I need to be mindful of the company I keep and be particularly aware when going for a night out and my behaviour in a work place, I have never really thought long and hard about the etiquette and what to do when looking for a place to live. My priority has usually been to find somewhere that is cheap, so when I stumbled across an advert that was cheaper than what I was paying for food weekly, I thought all my birthday's had come at once! However, on inspection, I realised that it was an apartment that had been set up like a hostel. There were seven people living in a two bedroom apartment, with two bunk beds in one room and a double and a single bed in the other.

At this time, I had been living in a hostel for several weeks and was getting a bit tired of people coming and going in the middle of the night, either from their flight or drunk. I often found myself having sleepless nights or disturbed sleep and found that the price per night for the pleasure of this experience was not particularly cheap. So taking the plunge to flat share seemed like the next best thing.

When I was at the apartment, I was quickly shown around while most people were out. I can say it was by no means perfect, but the rent was, which led me to say yes and move in that night. Little did I know that when I set my suitcase in the corner of the room that night, I was going to quickly learn that the double bed was mine and for me to share!

Thankfully, my bedmate worked night shifts and whilst everyone there were lovely, I did not stay long. That experience did however make me realise that the small print that I had taken for granted should always be observed, looked into, checked, then re-checked and triple checked before putting down deposits and taking semi-permanent actions that I may later regret!

NAIVETY IS THE SPICE OF LIFE

One sure thing is that my naivety has shone brightly on many occasions throughout my life. From dancing on stage and removed by drag queens, to watching the shoes I was about to buy at a Chinese market set on fire as "proof" of their genuine leather status to falling in love and making plans with a guy who two years later, announced that his wife had been arranged and it was time for him to go home.

There are some things in life I will never understand and I acknowledge the life I have is very different from other people's and the lens I view the world from will be very different as well. Amongst the awkwardness, the heart ache, the quick-thinking-stumble-for-an-action that prevents humiliation situation, I value the lessons I've learnt.

MORAL OF THE STORY

Do not take the things you know, experience, feel or do for granted. Do your homework, ask questions, take some time to think about the situation and reflect. Your world view can be completely different from someone else's and when you are overseas or around people from diverse backgrounds, you cannot take that you are all on the same page for granted. However different someone may appear, do your best not to judge as you have not walked in their shoes and have no idea what their life circumstances or experiences have been like. Sometimes, you will find yourself in situations where you all speak the same language but will not understand each other's words or actions. Sometimes, you will speak different languages and will make a connection that you never thought was possible but the cultural differences are too strong to ignore. Either way, this should not stop you from getting to know people because diversity is what makes life interesting. Learning about other people, their views and experiences of life, and what this means to them helps us grow into the person we are today.

Chapter 7:
Don't Rock The Boat

While overseas, you are likely to be exposed to things you would not normally come across at home. Sometimes, you will find yourself making random, unexpected, spur-of-the-moment decisions based on an opportunity that presents itself. It may not be something you would have purposely planned to do in any other circumstance, but because the moment arises, and you are away, you think why not; and as a result, you let your curiosity take the lead.

On one of my earlier trips to Cyprus, my brother, my best friend and I were casually walking past a travel agency and stumbled across an advert for a three-day cruise to Egypt for ninety nine pounds! The advert said it was due to leave the very next day and as we all looked at each other, we realised we did not need to waste any time trying to convince each other, so we hurried in to see if it was possible. Thirty minutes later, we had our tickets in our hands and knew that the next three days of our trip had been planned out!

None of us had been on a cruise before, let alone imagined we would be getting to see a glimpse of Egypt during this trip! What should we take with us? What did we already have? What did we need? I often compare my "tan" with the colour of self-rising flour, and unfortunately, go through a process of burning, peeling and going back to my fair skin again; so I was already fully prepared with half a suitcase of factor 50 sun cream! Getting burnt was not an option! However, I wondered if I should wear clothes that covered my arms and knees? How much walking would we be doing? Is packing for

Cyprus different from packing for Egypt? I had no idea! However, for a three-day trip, and a lesson already learnt from my oversized suitcase experience in Italy, it was easy to pack light! So we did exactly that and decided to go with the flow.

The next day, when we boarded the ship, we were excited. We had our tickets and our light luggage and had spent the previous night discussing all the amenities that we could use and explore on the ship in depth. The buffet food, the rooftop pool, the nightclub, the gym, the gift shops, the bar and the entertainment! Our first stop was our room and we found that it was a room without a porthole. As we explored our room, we laughed and joked at the fact that everything was firmly bolted down. The table, the chairs, the beds, the mirror and the pictures were all securely attached to either the floor or the wall.

We went upstairs and enjoyed the array of succulent sweets and savories on offer from the buffet and cheerfully sang along and listened to the live entertainment. Knowing that the ship would take all night to reach our destination and we only had one full-day in Egypt, we decided to go to bed early enough to ensure we felt nice and refreshed. While chatting, we tried to imagine what Egypt would be like before drifting off to sleep to the rhythmic motion of the sea, like a gentle lullaby.

Sadly, the lulling lullaby turned into a nauseous nightmare as rocky waters caused the ship to sway abruptly from side to side. Clambering to the bathroom, I made it just in time but while my tummy was now empty, it did not stop churning. Moments later, my brother and best friend follow suite and they are also looking a light shade of green and between us, we are scrambling to gain composure during a harsh shake up of the ocean. I would be lying if I said that was an easy night! By no means was it easy and when we finally made it safely to shore, my body continued to rock from side to side as if my whole being was still being shaken to its core.

Upon leaving the ship, I was greeted by an intensely overbearing dry heat that made my eyeballs sting. With every breath I took, I could feel the heat catch the back of my throat and nose. My sun cream was glistening as I witnessed my translucent skin turn a shade of pink. This was by far an experience of heat like I had never felt before.

Before jumping onto a wonderfully air-conditioned bus which was to take us to the pyramids and explore more of Egypt's wonderful sights, we first needed to wander through the market stalls. Children chanted welcome greetings in a number of different languages to gauge what country we were from. They then turned on their cheeky charm and uttered phrases familiar to that country. Our English one was "Buy one, get one free - it's cheaper than ASDA!"

Walking through the market stalls with no experience of the bartering system was slightly intimidating. I quickly found memorabilia being hurled my way from all directions, and anxiously panic buying plastic camels, Egyptian headpieces, more plastic camels, pictures, gemstones and again, yes, more plastic camels; just because I could not say no! I only stopped when I literally could not carry any more. I certainly had more than I wanted, needed or could have possibly asked for!

Although it was a very short trip, Egypt was an immensely interesting place to visit. My highlights were seeing the pyramids up close, learning about the mummification process, Tutankhamun, papyrus (material like thick paper which used to be used for writing on) and getting a glimpse into Egypt's history and culture. A day was not really long enough, however, the memory of the experience getting there was still so fresh that the dread of what was to come lay heavy in my stomach.

However, I was to fear no more as upon arrival at the cruise ship, motion sickness tablets were offered at the reception, to help me and others tackle the journey back to Cyprus! Oh what a difference this made! On the way back, we all managed to make it to the nightclub and requested the song "rock the boat" by the Hues Corporation and took turns to do the Michael Jackson moonwalk slide as the boat took us in one direction and then the next!

MORAL OF THE STORY

We may not always be prepared for opportunities that come our way, and chances are we won't have a crystal ball to tell us how the experience will turn out, but things like motion sickness tablets, sun cream, torches, money belts/pouches, first aid kits, plasters and hand sanitizer can all be organised before your trip and are useful accessories to have available on any trip you go on! Wear new shoes before taking them with you, if you intend to walk in them lots! Check the climate of the country you are going to and whether you need particular vaccinations before visiting. It is a whole lot easier to organise these things before you go overseas, particularly when you are in a country you are familiar with and know the language well. So do yourself a favour and be prepared to manage situations that you can prevent which will make life a whole lot easier!

CHAPTER 8:
THE CON TIMES AND THE UNLUCKY TIMES!

I've always believed that the company you keep and the stories you tell make experiences memorable. While they may not always be positive moments at the time, they tend to add richness to your experience and you can be sure to find a lesson in there!

Throughout my travel experiences, there have been a few times where I've found myself in situations that have made me realise that I am being targeted for money. Not in the sense where my wallet is at risk, (although this also does happen as we uncovered through the "one English Penny" scenario earlier!), but more so in the tactics played by others who are trying to get you to willingly hand over your cash.

TUKTUK TIME

One incident I remember clearly was when I decided to jump in a TukTuk (which is a three-wheeled vehicle that takes passengers around like a taxi; where the front part tends to look like a motorcycle). After chatting with the driver and talking through where I wanted to go, he offered to take me through a route that enabled me to see some of the sights. As he listed off the temples and other places of interest that he was offering to drive by, I found myself thinking that it sounded like quite a nice idea. I had heard that you needed to barter a price up front before jumping into the TukTuk and knowing this wasn't a strength of mine, I attempted to do this and we reached a reasonable agreement and settled on a price before I jumped in. I sat in the back feeling proud of myself for navigating the bartering system and pleased that I was able to see more than what I would have on foot.

As I heard the humming noise of the TukTuk's motor, I started to relax and enjoy the wind blowing through my hair as the air breezed through the sides of the vehicle while we navigated the windy streets. However, a few minutes into the journey the driver pointed over his head and said "we just need to stop in here for a petrol voucher". Shortly after, we pulled up into a large car park of a jewelry store. It was in this moment I quickly learnt (and of course had not anticipated), that the petrol voucher was dependent upon me going into the store and buying something.

At first, I was surprised to be asked as we had already bartered and agreed on the ride details and price, but I obliged and went into the store to see if I could help the TukTuk driver out. I swiftly realised that there was no way I could afford the prices that were on offer inside the store and scurried out empty handed. As you can imagine, this did not please the driver and he did not hide his feelings regarding this. I then found myself being taken to a number of different shops with the aim that I would, at some point, come back with a petrol voucher.

As I entered each shop, the same scenario would occur as I would take a look around, gasp at the price, make my way back to the TukTuk to be greeted by annoyance and anger and then driven to the next store! This went on for about half an hour while I tried to explain my situation which included travelling on a budget, but this was not accepted as the driver continuously pulled up into different shops for me to buy something for his voucher. Practicing my assertiveness, I continued to insist on cutting the journey short as I did not have the money to spend and requested to be taken to my final destination. While feeling stressed and frustrated, I left the TukTuk without spending money I did not have and eventually arrived safely at my destination.

IT'S TIME TO FLY THE NEST

Another time was when I was walking through a busy street in Thailand. Minding my own business, I was approached by a lady who was offering to sell some bird food, so that I could feed the birds in the park adjacent to me. I politely declined the offer, but as a result of this decline I was on the end of potential passive aggressiveness where the bird feed was thrown directly at me. You can only imagine what unfolded seconds later, although at the time I was blissfully unaware of the event that was going to occur. The swarm of pigeons swooped down and around me to peck away at the food that was provided to them with me at the centre, flustered and feeling under attack. Alarmed and upset that someone could orchestrate such a scenario, I thankfully came away unscathed and surprisingly managed to make my exit without any "lucky" bird poop on me to mark the occasion!

MORAL OF THE STORY

Travelling has been a lifestyle choice where I have consciously chosen to devote my working career to be able to fund the next adventure. This does not come without sacrifices or disadvantages as the "travel itch" can be so strong that staying in one location for very long can feel overwhelming because you are used to being on the go all the time and seeing different things which can inhibit other life choices such as having a family or buying a house. At the same time, having these travel experiences is a privilege, just like being able to have a family, own your own house or to have access to opportunities that others are not privy to.

While I have worked hard to be able to achieve my goals and tread my chosen path, I am privileged to have had the opportunity to work in countries that speak the same language and obtain work visas to be able to live and work in different areas. From the outside, for someone who comes from a different culture, lives by different cultural norms or has different country rules to follow, you may find yourself being seen as wealthy and a target for cons and scams. But as with anything in life, we only see from our lens and not the other person's. So while it is good to have your wits about you, be aware of the choices you have in life and remember that not everyone will be fortunate to have the circumstances to be able to walk in your shoes.

Be open to seeing a different story from the one you may first assume and have respect for diversity. Even while having pigeons invade my personal space and receiving hassle for not spending money that I didn't have, I was conscious that the life picture I saw was from the shoes that I, alone, walked in and although frustrating and unpleasant, they happened for reasons I'll never fully be aware of.

CHAPTER 9:
YOU BE YOU

Sometimes, when you are away or meeting new people, there will be parts of yourself that you may want to hide or are embarrassed about. It may be a fear you have or situations where you know you become irrational. Or it may be those unusual habits or quirks you display during particular times or it may just be something you are conscious of, like the way you pronounce particular words that others have laughed at in the past, making you super self-conscious!

For me, I have always been a bit scared of spiders. I can safely say they are my least favourite species and I have had more than my fair share of encounters that have frightened me. From working in a laundry factory and having a large furry one land on me from up above which made me desperately try to take my top off to get it away from me, to hearing a large spider crawl along one my posters in my bedroom when I was a teenager and finding it shortly before it approached my bed. As the years have passed by, I have become less afraid as I have learnt that the ones I have come across are harmless and are likely to be more scared of me than I am of them.

However, there was a time when I was travelling and participating in an overnight trek where my fear got the better of me. During the day, I had been wading through knee-deep water with eels swimming past my feet and water spiders scurried by. Although this made my heart beat faster, I managed to clamber to the other side and continue with the trek to the cabin we were staying at. The cabin was set up like a wooden shed, but the difference was it had a thatched roof, open sides and mosquito nets hanging from the roof to surround the thin mattresses to ensure we had have a pain-free night's sleep.

That night, cooking dinner took longer than it did for us to devour our creation, as we were quite hungry and just as tired. We appreciated the moment to enjoy the wide-open night sky which was filled with stars and shared travel stories and adventures before going to bed. As a bedtime ritual, one of the girls from the tour shone her torch light around the ceiling of our thatched roof and gave us a fright as she screamed at the sight of large, dark, furry creatures nestled in amongst the light coloured straw material above us. The girl dropped her torch and ran outside which led myself and others to take turns to shine the torch brightly on the spots above us to see for ourselves.

Huddled together outside, we were slightly terrified at the thought of sharing our space with these furry creatures but we eventually managed to calm each other down and took comfort in the mosquito nets being around us to shield us from any fall a furry friend may encounter. So one by one, we jumped into our sleeping bags and carefully placed the mosquito net around us so that we were out of harm's way.

Over the years, I've learnt that nervous energy can make you feel really sleepy and if you can rationalise a situation and calm yourself down, it is surprising how quickly you can fall into the deep trance of a good night's sleep. However, while rationalising a situation can help you in the present moment, it doesn't necessarily help your mind switch off. So while in my slumbering state, I found myself rolling over to feel something on my face. Of course, my instant reaction was to scream the place down as spiders were the last thing I saw before I closed my eyes to sleep. Apparently, I frantically shouted "it's on me, it's on me" in a grave, panic-stricken way which startled the whole cabin and led everyone to jump up and out of their beds.

Sadly, I have had a history of sleep talking over the years and when I looked around and noticed the utter chaos around me, I searched around my area for a large furry creature and quickly realised that I had likely just gotten a bit too close to the mosquito net and it had perhaps lightly touched my face. I apparently then decided to tell everyone that "all was okay, it was a false alarm" before snuggling into my sleeping bag to return to my slumber state, while the rest of the cabin were left to find their own way of bringing a sense of calm to their evening, so they too could reach their land of Zen. *Whoops! I am really sorry everyone!*

MORAL OF THE STORY

We all have quirky habits and fears, and for me, sleep talking and having a fear of spiders is a part of me. When travelling, only you know about these traits, until of course, circumstances cause you to unwillingly share them with others! But that is okay, we are only human and with that comes a range of emotions, quirks and personalities!

Over the years, I have learnt that I am a people pleaser. I want people to like me and I can find myself tip toeing around others to ensure they are happy and things are okay. Yet in situations like these, where I have behaved unconsciously and asleep, like this case - I've learnt that it is okay to be me! While my sleep talking incident may have annoyed pretty much everyone on the tour, and there may have been some grumpy people in the morning due to their lack of sleep, no-one held it against me. Even if they had, I also have the choice to mix and mingle with those people or not. Travelling is a great opportunity to find yourself and learn to be okay with who you are. We are all different, we are all learning, we are all in this world together trying to do the best we can. While it is important to care about others and apologise when wrong has been done (whether intentional or not), it is important to be true to yourself. I cannot control my sleep talking but perhaps in the future, I will only check for spiders if I can cope with the consequences!

CHAPTER 10:
WHEN THINGS GO SOUTH

When you travel, expect the unexpected, but sometimes, things happen that you could never have predicted. At the time of writing this, the world has been affected by a global pandemic known as COVID-19; a virus that has managed to contaminate pretty much the entire world. Countries have found themselves on "lockdown" to try and break the chain of transmission that has taken many lives and has impacted even more. Separated by oceans and continents, many of the world's borders have been closed and "social distancing" and "isolation bubbles" are new phrases that individuals around the world are trying to manage. Schooling is in the home, police officers are patrolling open spaces, supermarkets are working around the clock to replenish stock and essential workers are placed on the front line, to help the rest of the world function and stay safe. Everyone else stays home to prevent the virus from spreading to help save lives.

At this stage, no-one really knows what life will look like after COVID-19. However, during this time, while people are locked up indoors, the lack of traffic has lightened the air, the sound of birds can be heard more than before and wildlife are able to venture further because humans no longer block their path. At present, air traffic has been heavily reduced and policies and procedures will likely change to reflect the new world we have experienced, to keep the virus at bay and to keep us all safe. However, due to the global economy and the diverse placement of people spread around the world, when safe to do so, the act of travel itself is likely to continue on, to keep us all connected.

While travel challenges have always been there, they have perhaps been seen to be on more of an individual scale. I, for one, am no stranger to this!

On my trip to Australia (the one I briefly mentioned at the beginning of this book), I had a long bus ride ahead of me as I left Cornwall and headed to London. My flight was in the morning, so I left for my adventure in the middle of the night.

On entering the bus, people were taking up two seats as they sprawled across the chairs to find a comfortable position to fall asleep. As I walked down the aisle of the bus to try and see if there was a free seat, I was starting to panic as no spaces were available. Thankfully, a seemingly nice young man took pity on me and moved across so I could sit next to him. At first, I was appreciative of the gesture, but about 20 minutes or so into the journey, the passenger rested his head on my shoulder, snuggled up into me and wrapped his arms around me! A few digs with my elbow and the man awoke and apologised but sadly, this continued for the entire journey, keeping me on high alert and wide awake for the whole duration.

Tired from the long and stressful journey, I arrived at the airport to check in and was told that my electronic visa had not been processed. This of course was needed to be able to fly so I needed to get it organised before being able to check-in with my luggage. Thankfully, I was at the airport with enough time to seek assistance from staff (as this was before the days we had smart phones to help us access the internet and organise things quickly for ourselves). I was also really lucky that the visa was processed automatically as I have learnt from other travel adventures that some can take weeks to be processed and some need to be processed in person!

When I eventually managed to board the plane to Australia, it was probably the longest trip I have ever taken. While my ticket was pretty good value for money, it meant I had four stops along the way and each stop came with its own additional transit waiting time before I could board the next flight, making an on-average 40 hour door to door journey turn into a 50+ hour journey! This was a lesson I quickly learnt to consider and look into, when booking long haul flights!

DISAPPEARING ACT

There has also been another incident when I was told the flight I booked no longer existed! Thankfully, the travel agency recognised it was their mistake and organised a new ticket for me. This was extremely stressful time and can give you additional hassles that you need to try and sort out to make things work out for the best. However, I found that staff are particularly helpful if I remain calm. They have also been super helpful when they see that I have been travelling on my own and have done what they could to help me.

When things disappear, travel insurance can be a blessing! Thankfully, I have never had to use it but over the years, I've realised and appreciated the importance of travel insurance. When you are on a budget and saving hard for travel, it can be one of those items you think is wasted money and you may think you will be fine, you will not need it. But without it, you can find yourself spending a fortune on luggage replacement, medical/hospital fees or putting your family in the situation of having to pay for repatriation costs should anything dire happen to you while you are away.

Check the fine print to see what you are covered for and look at the details on your flight ticket to make sure you are not expected to call in the day before to confirm you will be using it.

It is also crucial to ensure the timings and dates on your ticket are correct as you can easily get confused especially if your flight is at midnight and you cannot tell which night you have to be at the airport. Most, if not all flights, will put this time as 11:59pm to help you avoid turning up at midday the next day! It is also good to be aware of Daylight Savings Time if your flight is due to leave on a day the clocks change as setting alarms on clocks that do not automatically update can cause problems for you as well!

IS THIS YOUR BAG, MA'AM?

I have to say, out of all of my travel experiences, the most stressful to date has been when I was meeting my brother in Bali. We had not seen each other for over a year so were organising a "half-way" catch-up and had found flights that arrived 30 minutes apart from each other. He was flying from the UK and I from New Zealand and my flight was due to leave at 5am which meant I was up at 1am and at the airport by 2am.

When I arrived at the airport, the check-in was like it always was, although I recall being at the front of the queue so there was no waiting around! I checked in and headed straight through border control which I remember being happy about because it was really quick and smooth. I sat in the departure lounge waiting area and took out my headphones to listen to my favourite tracks. My mind not yet switched off, I decided to call my brother to let him know how excited I was to be seeing him soon! We briefly chatted but I learnt he was about to board his flight (which was from the other side of the world) so in our excited voices we said, "see you soon" and hung up. I tried to sit still but had lots of excited energy that I did not quite know what to do with. So I put my headphones back on and swayed to the sounds of my favourite tunes while I waited to board the plane.

When I boarded the plane, I switched off my phone. I normally request for the window seat so I can fold up a jumper and rest my head in the window area to get some sleep, but I was not yet tired so I flicked through the pages of the in-flight magazine to read some of the articles instead. Leading up to this trip, I had been working long hours so it is always nice when you sit on the plane and take a deep breath and let out a sigh of relief that you have made it. Still restless and excited, I smiled to myself and grabbed the headphones and started scrolling through some of the music albums to see if there was anything new that I could test out. Leaning back into my seat, I put the magazine away and closed my eyes to enjoy the rhythmic music to put me in the mood for my adventure.

Then, out of no-where, I felt a tap on my shoulder. I looked up to see the air steward standing over me. I took my headphones away from my ears to hear her words and quickly learnt that she was asking me for my name. I reluctantly told her and was then asked to come with her. In doing so, I was taken to the doors of the plane where she pointed to my luggage and said "Is this your bag ma'am?" My heart sank. It was. A surge of panic came over me as a flashback of a TV episode came to my mind. Someone was on a trip to Bali and had drugs planted in their bag. The person who owned the bag was set up and was immediately thrown in jail. A wave of fear rolled over me. Had someone planted drugs in my bag? Breaking my thoughts, the air steward again asked "Is this your bag, Ma'am?" I sheepishly said "yes" terrified of what that might mean for me but also trying to recall who I had crossed paths with on my way to the airport.

The air steward then went on to inform me that I would not be travelling today.

Confused, overwhelmed and in shock, I asked why, to be told that my passport was not in date. I was flying on 8th September and my passport was to expire on the 7th of March the following year. Entering into a debate that took me around in circles, for what felt like ages, I was escorted off the plane because I had a passport that was one day less than the required six months validity. I was away for about a week and had a return flight but apparently, that was not adequate. I had to sign paperwork for my "off-boarding" experience and was told if I had flown, I would have had police waiting for me in Bali and I would have been sent back home. If I wanted to travel to Bali, I needed to organise a new passport.

I felt like a criminal as I was escorted out of the airport. I was frustrated by the whole experience and livid with all the free time I had in the airport before boarding the plane and also by the fact that I was allowed to check-in my luggage and board the plane to begin with! I had been waiting at the departure lounge for a long time and had I not been allowed to board the plane, I may have been able to organise my emergency passport in the time I had, which is something I guess, I will never know. Devastated, deflated and down-right annoyed, I signed paperwork, hopped on a bus and made my way into the city to find the office that would provide me with an emergency passport.

On the way, I attempted to call my brother, but since he had already left, I left voicemail, internet based and text messages for him in the hope he would pick at least one of them up when he arrived in Bali.

As it was still early in the morning when I arrived at the Passport office, they were not open so I had to queue outside and wait. However, they were amazing when they opened their doors to me and were extremely helpful with organising my new passport within a few hours. I had planned to meet a friend in Australia and spend the day with her before flying onto Bali, so I started to regain hope that I could book another flight to Australia and still make it in time for my connecting flight to Bali.

While waiting for my passport, I called travel agents to get advice on my situation and ask if they had any flights to Australia that I could take so that I could make my connecting flight. They were surprised at my situation and said that it should not have happened, yet were unable to help me because I was in the process of reorganising a passport and I was in the system for being offloaded from the plane, meaning questions would be asked as to why I am desperately trying to get to Bali which might delay me further.

When I received my passport, I called the original airline to get their advice on using my Australia to Bali ticket and was pertly told "madam, you were a no-show this morning, therefore, your ticket has been cancelled".

Tired, stressed, overwhelmed and frustrated, I explained what had happened and was told I could not fly again until the next day. I was also told that I had to pay for another ticket. Trapped in a situation I had no control over, I begrudgingly gave my credit card details to pay for the ticket which took up most of the spending money I had saved for the trip.

Heading home with a heavy heart and tears in my eyes, I contacted the accommodation and taxi bookings I had made for myself and my brother to let them know that even though the bookings were in my name, it would only be my brother who would be using them for the first night. I informed them all of the situation, in the hope that someone would be able to communicate this to my brother in case he was not able to see his messages while waiting for me to arrive.

I did not sleep at all that night, until I received a message from my brother to let me know that he had arrived safely and had received my messages. Then, my alarm went off at 1am and I repeated my ritual to get to the airport with my new passport. I hate photographs at the best of times but this particular passport photograph tells its own story and will be a constant reminder for the next 10 years until it is time for renewal!

MORAL OF THE STORY

So much in life can be beyond your control. It is hard to prepare for the unexpected and even more so, when you feel like you are a seasoned traveller and come across something that no one has ever talked of or mentioned before, or perhaps has never happened before. The COVID-19 pandemic has highlighted the importance of checking travel news and websites, getting travel insurance and keeping in touch with others.

When I first started travelling, I booked everything through a travel agent; but it was in these situations that I found myself in the rare situation of being booked on a flight that did not exist and my accommodation was organised via commercialized resorts rather than in the heart of an area where you experienced a true culture of a place. However, when I organised my trip to Bali, I booked the flights online (like I had for so many other flights that were fine), but on this particular occasion, a travel agent may have perhaps warned or alerted me to the situation with my passport. Or perhaps not, I guess this is something I will never know.

It is important to recognise that times are changing, therefore, it is best to keep yourself informed and up to date with as much travel news and information as you can.

As a starting point, a range of websites have been listed at the back of this book to help keep you informed so that you can stay up to date when you are taking trips overseas.

CHAPTER 11:
THE MEMORIES A CAMERA CANNOT CAPTURE

It may be hard to appreciate, as the news around us is often filled with sadness and fearful stories, but the world is full of beautiful sights and experiences if we are open to seeing them.

These sights are not always the kind a camera can capture, they are the moments that take your breath away. They are the moments that encapsulate every positive feeling and emotion you can feel at once, and they are the moments that radiate a scene or an essence in time, so magical that they become imprinted in your mind forever.

ANIMALS

Just like a TV host's rule "never work with animals or children" (due to their unpredictable nature), - capturing the true essence of these moments can be hard. Yet, how much time have we actually spent watching animals from afar? They often move fast and can behave unexpectedly, but they also have a wonderful way of portraying innocence, along with highlighting the circle of life and the hierarchical nature of the world we live in.

One of my favourite moments while travelling was a time when I was in Tasmania on a tour to see the penguins. We were taken to a National Park situated by the sea. The night sky was lit in all its glory with the stars sparkling around us and the soft sound of the ocean gently whispering in the background. We waited in anticipation as the night air wrapped itself around us and moments later, shadows scurried across the sand. Making their way towards us, little penguins delightfully appeared at our feet, before roaming past us to make it back to their homes. The feeling of that moment would be hard to capture in words and pictures as catching a glimpse into their world was so enchanting and so exciting. Hurriedly moving together as a large group; waddling along the sand, a memory I will never forget and one that no camera could truly capture!

MONKEY BUSINESS

I have also been lucky enough to witness the moment where a monkey, who was resting on a tree branch, held up its hands and caught a butterfly! The monkey then went on to delicately play with it, moving it from hand to hand and inspecting it, before letting it go so that the butterfly could spread its wings and fly away. A rare and priceless moment I have been wonderfully privileged to see.

In discussions over that moment, the fact that the butterfly did not appear to be harmed, has been pondered. Even though at first glance, you would have thought that the monkey would have been clumsy and have damaged the butterfly's delicate wings or body in some way, this was not the case. The monkey, although playing what appeared to be a game, was curious and careful. It is this perspective that has helped me not only become more observant around nature, but also more appreciative of the animal kingdom around us as I do not believe we, as humans, give them the credit they deserve.

PEOPLE

While travelling, you will also come across people who will touch your mind and heart. One of the most beautiful moments I can remember, which I hold close to my heart, is the time when I was working in an orphanage. A young child, who must have been about two years old would greet me every morning with a smile that lit up the entire room. He would give larger-than-life chuckles at the bubbles I would blow and him, and the other children would chase, pop and play the game which would often be stuck on repeat as the air filled with joyful moments.

Language was a barrier for myself and the toddlers, and in my time with them, I only heard the children speak two English words. One was "Up" to be lifted-up to look out the window or out of their cot and the other was "Mamma" - which they called every person that walked into the room. With this in mind, it was common for us to communicate through actions and expressions. However, this particular child, a beautiful soul, had his own ritual he would follow through each day as he would calmly walk over to me, take my hand and place my palm to his lips to gently kiss and make the "Mwaaah" sound. A moment in time, that melted my heart and will stay with me forever.

SCENES

Then, there have been times when mother nature has shared its beauty with me and I have been lucky enough to have been there to witness it, in all its glory.

Admittedly, at the beginning of my traveller days, I did not really do much planning or preparation. I would join a tour and then go with the flow as to whatever they were offering. I never did any research, and never had any expectations of what the day had in store for me. There was one trip, that stands out in my mind. I decided to join a tour because the rest of the group were going along, and I didn't fancy being on my own for the day. I did not really have any idea what it was all about, but was told to take enough food, and drink for the entire day and to wear walking shoes. I did not have any decent walking boots or shoes, so went along with my trainers and filled my rucksack with snacks, water and lunch. I do not know if my mind had been prepared for what was to come; whether I would have enjoyed it more, or whether I would have still gone along. But the trip ended up being an intense 19km alpine hike, that saw me climbing nearly 800m in altitude to 1900m above sea level, and required a good level of fitness - which at that particular time of my life, I did not have.

The hike started with a steep climb which lasted a lifetime, and I regularly had to stop to catch my breath. It was an intense eight-hour hike which left me unable to walk properly for three days afterwards! I did however keep going and with each step I felt tortured, as I had to hold on tight, and push myself up, and find my footing to keep climbing upwards. At the half-way point, I had taken off my jacket, and put my jacket back on, a dozen times. I had drank all my water and eaten all my food. But at that half-way point, I was enlightened to why so many people venture out, and attempt the hike that leaves such an imprint on your soul.

As I climbed to the top, I looked over and saw the most beautiful colours I had ever seen nature bring me. Lakes so pure, the sky so blue, the mountains so rugged. Standing high above the ground, looking over across the landscape, feeling every inch of your body as you have tried, and tested your endurance and grit which was oh, so satisfying. A feeling that no camera could capture in all its grandiosity. A truly breath taking moment, that has to be felt to be fully appreciated.

The second half of that hike was extremely harrowing as the ground crumbled away as I tried to make my descent. Awakening muscles I had no idea existed. Coming down was by far the harder mission.

Unpredictable weather can make the hike tough, and layers were needed. I had a warm jacket and a few layers, but my trousers were cropped at the knees, and my trainers thankfully had some grip left on them. Looking back, it was irresponsible of me to put myself, and others in the position I did by joining the tour with no idea of what I was getting myself into, and with the level of fitness I had.

MORAL OF THE STORY

I consider myself extremely lucky to have been able to experience the experiences I have. But I cannot stress enough how important it is, to do your research. I came away unscathed from my hike, but others have not been as lucky. Being prepared, having the right equipment, food supplies, clothes and fitness levels are crucial for participating in activities that can be unsafe if essential information, and advice is not followed.

In this day and, age we live in, it is also be easy to believe that you will create that perfect camera shot if you just positioned yourself in a different spot, one that perhaps is not on the beaten track. While you may believe that is the case when you are in the moment, those tracks are put in place for your safety, and taking a detour can make you harder to be found if you were to find yourself in an unsafe situation, and needed to be rescued. Nobody is going to appreciate, nor enjoy those moments or photographs if you are no longer around to be the one to share them with others.

Therefore do what you can to make yourself, and others safe, do your research, follow the advice given, stay on the beaten track, tell people where you are going, and be sensible when trying to capture that perfect picture. The rules are there to protect you, and those opportunities can only stay open for us if we abide by the rules so that we can appreciate, and enjoy what the world has to offer.

CHAPTER 12:
SOCIAL RESPONSIBILITY

We, humans have neglected the world, and all that live within it. We litter, we pollute the air with our man-made machines and technologies, we waste food and we take each other for granted. We can become so caught up in consumerism and success that we lose sight of people, nature and what was here before we left our imprint on the world.

It can be hard to see this, as we live our lives this way day in, and day out. Travelling however, really opens up your eyes. This can sometimes surprise you, as you are faced with a reality different than what you expected. There have been trips, and tours that I have been on that have come from a place of curiosity. My heart has been in the right place, but the reality has seen me witness, and experience situations and circumstances that could be considered unethical. You can find yourself torn, because when you are in another country, you start seeing the world through a different set of lens as you try to see the other perspective. Activities, and experiences can also be marketed well, that they shine their best light on what it is they are offering, that you may be blindsided by awe until you see what is really in front of you.

My experience of volunteering in an orphanage is an example. On one hand, these children are in care, they require volunteers to support the paid workers so that the children receive individualized play, attention and support. The care-givers often find themselves operating on a production line system. Particularly for the babies where care-givers prepare food and then need to individually feed each baby, change their nappies and meet their needs. When one child cries, they all start to cry, so each has to be held and nurtured. Yet, when the room they are in is full of babies and, there is little attention to go round to them all, the child learns that their cries are meaningless which can mean that it stops. This then puts a halt to any form of stimulation, which can slow down the development process and becomes harmful for these children.

When physically inside the orphanage, with very little English being spoken, you make assumptions about what it is you see. Donations of books and toys sat high up on shelves out of reach of the children, only one child per volunteer to play outside in the winter, and the children seemingly desperate to be that one child each day.

One can only assume that volunteers are needed, these children require care, and attention to meet individualized needs. Play is a natural, and much needed part of child-development as it generates a number of opportunities for children to be curious, make connections and explore the world they live in.

However, on that trip I learnt that some of the children in the orphanage have parents who are alive. Poverty, and difficult life circumstances has seen these children placed in orphanages as a way to protect them, and give them a better life. Yet, in some instances, orphanages have been reported to have been set up as a way to profit from volunteers whilst taking advantage of vulnerable families to use their children as a way to do this.

When I left the orphanage, I did so with a heavy heart. I worried that I was another person who had abandoned these children, and I was contributing to a systemic cycle that repeatedly failed these children. But, how does one help fix it? Is it better to have contributed and provided care and support for a short time as opposed to not at all? Is it better that these children are there together in one place, that they have each other, and are amongst children of similar situations and circumstance? What is really going on within the orphanage, and within the country that sets this up? How can this be found out, and what needs to be done to change the system? I don't know the whole picture and unfortunately do not have the right answer, but I know that while I was there, I did all that I could to enrich the children's experiences. We played and had fun. During those times the children appeared happy. However, there are always two sides to every story, and when you are from a different culture, and speak a different language you may find yourself piecing together a picture that you are not sure quite fits.

Another example of experiences that I have been a part of which I would think twice about now, is visiting animals in enclosed spaces. On a trip to Thailand, I visited a tiger enclosure that held the promise of getting up close to view a tiger. I certainly got that, but sadly the tiger was in chains, and appeared lifeless which led me to question whether the tiger had been drugged for my viewing "pleasure".

Then there are times where you can find yourself viewing animals that are in spaces that restrict them from roaming free or are enslaved for your enjoyment such as riding elephants or camels. As a tourist, we fund these to continue to function. While many places care, and protect animals; some may have even rescued animals and nurtured them back to health so that they can then return to the wild. However, you can also find on the other end of the spectrum animals, and children cruelly taken advantage of, neglected, mistreated and harmed for profit making purposes.

MORAL OF THE STORY

As a traveller you are going to be curious, and you will want to explore, and find out what is on offer. If you participate in volunteer travel, do as much research as possible into what it is you are interested in doing including the organisation you are looking to go with. Find out what their viewpoints are; are they a reputable organisation that are geared up to provide responsible travel situations and experiences? Google them, what information can you find? What reviews have been left? What are other travellers saying? What are newspapers saying? We now live in a world where the internet is at our fingertips, we have access to information. Think about, and research what it is you are signing up for. What is it that is being offered, and at what cost, to those that are involved in the process?

CHAPTER 13:
RELATIONSHIPS

Love, and hate are two contrasting emotions that achieve two different outcomes. You can spend endless mediocre moments sitting on the edge of emotions, not intensely happy, but in the same breath not succumbing to the insatiable strain of sadness. Just peering into, over or through something that feels so intangible, so far away. The feeling of a lukewarm heart that hasn't hardened with ice nor threatened to bubble over as it overheats; it instead just beats and looks grey.

Love can fill a room. It can make you feel light. Like you are in a secure bubble that wraps its arms around you, and whispers in your ear "all *is well,* you've got this". The impossible begins to feels possible, it feels achievable as you are gently nudged towards being the best version of yourself. You do the things that make you happy, you feel inspired and this newfound confidence enables you to radiate positive energy, so much so, that people who pass by you, feel it too. Like a chain reaction, it is there at every turn; you feel amazing, you are invincible, this is wonderful.

Where there is light, there will always be darkness, and when you feel this inner positivity, it may stir up a lot of ugly emotions in others. You can find yourself on the receiving end of intense negative feelings towards you, without an understanding of why or how this happened. It can creep up fast, and can leave its mark on you as you try and piece parts of the puzzle together, and retrace your steps through the breadcrumb trail that leads you to where you are today.

The connections I have had with travellers have been amazing. We have been on the same page, we have had a thirst for adventure, we thrive off the adrenalin and the energy bounces around you as you are enthralled by the new sights, scenes, and experiences. Recounting the twists and turns; the predictable and unexpected; the "what-if's" and "can't believes", you enjoy sharing the moments with each other. Travelling helps me to feel in the zone, time passes me by without a recognition for anything as I am taken away, and consumed by the moment!

Like with all contrasting things in the world, can you really appreciate one end of the continuum, without also having experienced the other? Can you truly be happy if you have not experienced sadness? Just like we appreciate the rain when it has been missing for weeks, as the soil dries up and the luscious green disappears. Travelling is like the weather- it is not shining and bright forever. It is the bits in between that have found me on the receiving end of power play dynamics, bullying in the workplace or taking on jobs that I would not normally consider solely because I wanted to be able to fund the next adventure.

Building relationships can be hard when you travel as you flit from one place to another. Some workplace cultures are welcoming, and value an outsider's perspective where you will be included in meetings and treated as part of the team. While other times you may just be the temp that sits in the corner who is there to complete the task in hand, and have work delegated to without an utterance of small talk or niceties.

Making meaningful connections with people you trust, and relate to is important in any circumstance, however if you are travelling, and are going to be in an area for a reasonable length of time it is important you stay connected; having friends, and acquaintances to keep you going through the rough, and the smooth times. It is also important to have goals so that you do not succumb to basing your whole sense of worth on the tasks that you are involved in. Having a healthy relationship towards yourself is also important so that your mind is kind, and you are open to seeing the world as full of possibilities and opportunities.

Some of my saddest moments while travelling have been when I have not had anyone to share the highs and the lows with. This has taught me that I am my own cheerleader. I have had to give myself a "pep" talk or encourage myself to put in the effort to do something that I may not fully want to do but have committed to doing. Or I may need to give myself a boost by purposely doing something I enjoy, to avoid the negative energy I have been around from rubbing off on me. When I am working towards my goals, I often find it is the "end goal" that keeps me going, along with being kind to myself, and taking time out to enjoy the moments with people who have good energy, and care about me.

This of course is normally dependent on being in a good place and frame of mind, as my wellbeing cup needs to be full to be able to work at my best, and to be resilient to what life is throwing me. There have been times during my traveller days where I have gone against gut instincts because my wellbeing cup has been low. Instances where I have known, deep down that the invitation extended to me was not going to make me feel good about myself nor have my best interests at heart. Where I have gone along anyway and have allowed other people to get to me, and rock my sense of self-worth. However, my sense of self can only be rocked if I let it, and this is normally the case when it is a bit wobbly to start with. So with this, I aim to have a balanced life so that my wellbeing cup is full to overflowing. For me, this means I am active, and I am able to enjoy the outdoors, where I might see the sea, or trees or the moon. It is when I am working towards my goals and keeping my mind active and when I have healthy relationships, and doing things I enjoy. Being in a balanced state allows my wellbeing cup to be overflowing so that I can put the best version of myself forward and have the capacity to help others.

When I am in this place mentally, I am emotionally secure, and happy. However, when my life is not balanced, it is like my wellbeing cup has holes in it. I can focus on one thing such as working and saving but my enjoyment for life can deteriorate because I have neglected other important parts of my life. It is not always easy to get the balance right as everything is so connected. You may rely on money to be able to afford to socialize with friends or you may become ill that makes it harder to be active. Sometimes you need to find creative ways to make up for it. Like recording silly videos of yourself and sending them to family back home. Or listening to music; closing your eyes, visualizing how good it feels doing what you enjoy, that it feels like you are actually there already doing it.

MORAL OF THE STORY

Travelling can inspire, and fuel the thrill seeker in you, although the bits in between can be mediocre or dull as you build up to being in that future position of experiencing an adventure. Sometimes while we are in the bits in-between we can crave to belong and look for love in the wrong places to try and fill the void.

Over the years I have learnt that building a relationship with yourself will be the best thing you can do. It helps you learn about what you enjoy, the things that make you tick, the person you are, and the person you want to be. By making time to find out about yourself, you start to build a picture of what is important to you which helps you in all aspects of your life. You will not always get a choice of who you work with, or come into contact with, but if you have a healthy relationship with yourself, you can do more to protect yourself against those unhappy people who radiate jealousy and negativity, and you can instead focus on finding your tribe.

If you do not already know the ingredients required to fill that wellbeing cup of yours, I dare you to find out, so that your wellbeing cup overflows, and you can show the best version of yourself; as there is no better feeling than radiating joy for the life you are living and loving. A questionnaire and action plan have been provided at the back of this book to help you get started.

Chapter 14:
Reflection, Meaning, Purpose and Achievement

As a young girl embarking on a travel journey that started in her late teens, there were elements of naivety, common-sense, rebellion and a care-free attitude mixed into the days of exploring the unknown. In my early traveller days, I was amazed at how I could meet people from all around the world who spoke English as their first language, yet our dialects and accents saw us constantly searching our brain to try, and figure out what had just been said!

I learnt so much from the people and places I visited. With every person and experience carrying a special place in my heart.

When I set off for my first adventure all of those years ago, I had no idea how much the experience would change my life and as a result of those experiences, the reflections and personal growth I have done, I feel I am a confident, well-rounded individual that has respect, patience, empathy, and understanding of the people I encounter.

Travelling is not always easy, there will be many times where you question yourself, and your ability to do something you thought you really wanted to do. You will encounter various personalities, and different modes of thought, but the one thing travel will bring you is an array of colourful experiences, stories and memories that are likely to stay with you forever.

In summary, here are few key take home messages:

- Find strategies to make those everyday uncomfortable situations easier to handle.
  Learn about yourself; experiment with what works for you.
  Make the adjustments and grow from the experiences.

- Be kind to yourself, reflect and acknowledge how far you have come no matter how small you may feel it is. If you could not do it yesterday but did it today, you have come a long way. If you have learnt something that you did not previously know, you are moving forward.

- Have the courage to be who you are. If there is something you have always wanted to try, but there is something niggling away at you that is holding you back, identify what is stopping you. The chances are, they are the fears of the unknown. People rarely regret giving something a try. Think about it, have you ever heard someone say: I wish I did not do that skydive or I wish I did not go on that trip? No matter how fearful you may be, have faith that it will work out okay, and think about how amazing you will feel when you have achieved it, or when you have gone out there, and given it a go!

- There is no shame in having sad days when life feels like it should be amazing. Some days will be tougher than others but try not to wait for things to get really bad before reaching out. Learn about yourself so you can plan ahead and recognise your own warning signs that you need to look after yourself more. Practice self-care and be kind to yourself and get enough sleep.

Find ways that work for you, which may be writing in a journal, getting out in nature, taking photographs, drawing, doing some exercise or calling family and friends. Acknowledge your courage, and have compassion for yourself and others, setting yourself up so that you have a support system in place, readily there for when you may need it.

- Travelling can be expensive, but you can still have a fantastic time on a low-cost budget. Experiences, and memories often outweigh physical possessions or memorabilia. The greatest of adventures often start from the mind!

- Think about the items you may need that you can organize, and pack just in case the need arises. Things like motion sickness tablets or wrist bands, mosquito repellant, and headache tablets are all items that can be easily purchased in the country you are in before you leave. This will help you avoid needing to recognise brand names, or foreign words to meet the needs of the situation you may find yourself in. Money belts, separate wallets, sun cream, wearing in shoes before you go anywhere, are also things we can take for granted when we are in our own country, but can find yourself in the predicament of being in pain or in the scenerio of being poor if they are not planned for in advance.

- Being on an adventure away from family and friends can be hard, particularly when you are not around loved ones when they are in need. The distance between you can feel larger than life itself and the guilt you may carry for not being there can eat away at you. People may try to protect you from learning about the events taking place back home, and you too may try to do the same. While we are all on different paths, staying connected, and communicating with each other can help bridge the emotional gap when the physical distance feels overwhelmingly large.

- Every photo tells a story, but it may not be the picture that is being displayed. Remember to have fun, and enjoy the adventure! Some days will be better than others, but each day brings with it a new memory, a new chance for a new beginning or a new chapter of self-discovery!

- Check the small prints for timings, time zone, daylight savings and the actual airport. You do not want to be caught unaware that the large city you have just arrived in has more than one airport, and your accommodation is closer to the other one or you have arrived at the wrong airport for your departing flight.

- Embrace, respect and learn from diversity. Speak up if you are unsure, ask questions, and do not take for granted what you see from your perspective, cultural background and experiences will be the same as another person's. Think about situations and look to learn from one another.

- Be comfortable being you. Our quirks, strengths, weaknesses, skills, personality and habits are all what make us unique. As long as, our usual self is not setting out to hurt others, then relax and be proud of who you are. Life is hard enough as it is, without the burden of you having your own personal critic to battle with. No one is perfect, be true to yourself. You are special, unique and are at your optimum best when you can own it.

- However, if you are finding yourself setting out to hurt others then take a long hard look at yourself, and try to figure out what it is that is causing this. Chances are you are not happy. What can you do to change this? What makes you smile? If you do not know, try some new things and take some time to find out. Who is it you want to be? Who do you admire? What traits do they have that you would like to see in yourself? What steps do you need to take to change things for yourself? Who can help you on your journey to getting there?

- Smile, relax and appreciate the life you are blessed with. So many people in the world have their lives cut short. Their family, friends and selves would no doubt wish for one more day, one more memory, one more smile, one more moment. Live in the moment, make each of them count, be kind to yourself, be kind to others, live your life and love your life. You get one chance at life: what can you do to make it count?

CHAPTER 15:
MAKING THINGS HAPPEN

- ➤ Research what you want to do, and where you want to go. (See My Bucket List template)
- ➤ Speak with those that have already done it, and learn from them or from blogs on the internet.
- ➤ Research your options
  E.g. volunteering, couch surfing, tours, holiday, vacation with friends, working holidays.
- ➤ Research how much money you will need
  E.g. flights, accommodation, visa's, vaccinations, insurance, food, transport, tours, activities, sight-seeing entrance costs, spending money.
- ➤ Make a plan for what you want to do, and what you are going to do to make it happen.
- ➤ Is this realistic?
- ➤ Can you cut down on costs to save faster (e.g. reduce spending on coffee, clothes and nights out?).
- ➤ Are there cheaper alternatives? (E.g. backpacker Dorm shares instead of a hotel? All-inclusive tour packages instead of doing it yourself so you know what your costs are?).
- ➤ Plan ahead, have your goal in mind and keep saving!

My Bucket List

Things I have always wanted to do/see/explore/try/experience	Where can I do this?	Realistic timeframe to achieve this

PLANNING TEMPLATE

Flights	Cost	Savings goal
Accommodation	Cost	Savings goal
Visas needed	Cost	Savings goal
Vaccinations	Cost	Savings goal
Insurance	Cost	Savings goal
Transport	Cost	Savings goal
Food	Ave cost per day	Savings goal

Entry costs	Ave cost per day	Savings goal
Tours	Cost	Savings goal
Spending money	Cost per day	Savings goal

Note: The savings goal tends to be more than the cost you have found. This accommodates for the fluctuation of price and unexpected events or additional costs.

ACTIVITY IDEAS

Activity	Where	Cost	Savings goal

SAVINGS SACRIFICE TEMPLATE

My spending habits are:

E.g. coffee / take-aways / taxi / clothes / night's out etc.

Name of spending habit	Approx cost of spending habit	If I removed this habit or reduced the number of times during a week, I would save	If I removed this habit or reduced the number of times during a month I would save

USEFUL TRAVEL ACCESSORIES

Depending on what type of trip you may be going on, a list of potentially useful travel accessories can be found below.

- Sun cream
- Sunglasses
- Mosquito repellant
- Thermals
- Hat, scarf, gloves, rain-coat
- Comfortable worn-in shoes to walk long distances in
- Motion sickness tablets
- Headache tablets
- Water purifying products
- Torch
- Money belt/pouch
- Hand sanitizer
- First aid kit
- Additional wallet to store some of your cash in
- Padlock for your rucksack
- Sleeping sheet
- Portable clothes line (with suction or hooks on the end to hand wash and dry clothes on the go).
- Small light drawstring bag as laundry bag for underwear
- Light weight microfiber travel towel
- Travel hairdryer
- Toothbrush cap to protect head of toothbrush
- Ear plugs
- Mints/sweets to suck on in case your plane does not offer them for when you land.

Useful Websites

International Travel Updates and advice

- Check your local government website e.g.
  https://www.gov.uk/foreign-travel-advice
  https://www.safetravel.govt.nz/

World Health Organisation

- https://www.who.int/

Visa regulations

- Check your local government website e.g.
  https://www.gov.uk/standard-visitor-visa/apply
  https://www.immigration.govt.nz/new-zealand-visas/apply-for-a-visa

Vaccinations

- Check local government websites on the recommendations for the countries you are visiting or your local Dr.

Travel insurance

- Check large organisational brand names available to you from your home country e.g.
  https://www.ami.co.nz/travel-insurance

Chapter 16:
Finding Ways to Ensure Your Wellbeing Cup is Overflowing...

Step 1: Learn all about yourself!

I am most happiest when......

_____

This is because.....

_____

The last time I belly laughed was when......

_____

Laughing so hard made me feel.....

_____

My favourite time of year is.....

_____

This is when....

_____

My favourite animal is.....

_____

I love the way they.....

_____

My friends always come to me for.....

_____

I would say this is a strength of mine because....

_____

I go to my friends/family when I feel/need/....

_____

They help me because......

_____

If I was travelling and the time zone was not right, meaning I could not rely on friends/family to help me during a particular time, what steps could I take to help myself?

_____

_____

What would my friends/family say to me that I can tell myself?

_____

What activities do I enjoy doing?

_____

If I do not know, what would I like to find out and explore doing?

_____

_____

Am I okay with my own company or do I operate best around lots of people?

_____

_____

What do I need to recharge my energy (e.g. introverts tend to need time to themselves to restore their energy, they may enjoy writing or reading a book and having some quiet time. Extroverts often need to be around other people to recharge, they can feel re-energised by an interactive environment). What steps can I take to ensure I get this time for myself?

What parts of nature do I enjoy the most? (E.g. Walking in a park around trees, being with animals, seeing the sea, being in the sea, being in the air, seeing the moon and the night sky).

_____

_____

What can I do to ensure I get to enjoy nature around me?

_____

_____

Are you creative?   Do you like to paint/draw/take photographs etc...

_____

_____

Are you hard on yourself? How can you turn this around?

E.g. if you are often negative, find the positive in what you are doing or trying to do. Think of the courage, strength, and grit it takes to do something different, to break away from the norm. If it does not go well the first time, do not beat yourself up, you tried and that is amazing.

_____

_____

STEP 2: WHAT ACTION STEPS CAN YOU TAKE TO HELP YOURSELF

Homesickness can kick in at the beginning of any trip, particularly if you are new to a culture and way of life. Be kind to yourself. Check in with friends and family, but also make the effort to enjoy what your new area has to offer. You may also be jetlagged and exhausted from the journey. Things tend to be and feel a lot better after a good night's sleep.

> ➤ Organise regular zoom/WhatsApp chat/email interaction with friends and family to stay connected.
> ➤ Write in a journal - this can help you articulate your thoughts and feelings and can make you feel better.
> ➤ Think about the creative habits you can include in your life (photography, drawing, writing etc.).
> ➤ Think about the habits or activities you can take part in that is around nature and people with good energy.
> ➤ Aim to get good sleep and to protect yourself from not getting good sleep.
> ➤ Junk food can often be cheaper than healthier food, but your body will not thank you for it. It can impact your mood, sleep, digestion and can contribute towards an unhealthy viewpoint of yourself. Find ways to nurture yourself and fuel up on nutritious food.
> ➤ Recognise any negative thought patterns and aim to turn it around so that you are kinder to yourself. You are unique - the world is lucky to have you in it!

MY ACTION PLAN

Things that make me happy	How I can make this a habit

STEP 3: RECOGNISE YOUR STRENGTHS AND QUALITIES

My strengths and qualities are	I can utilize these by...

STEP 4: APPRECIATE ALL THAT YOU HAVE TO BE GRATEFUL FOR

My Gratitude List	
I am grateful for... because.... E.g. I am grateful for the food that nourishes my body I am grateful for the friends and family I have who care about me I am grateful to be able to do/see/experience/feel etc...	

STEP 5: CHALLENGE YOURSELF TO DO THREE THINGS EVERY DAY THAT MAKE YOU SMILE

This needs to be simple so that you can do it without depending on anyone else. Things like do a silly dance, speaking in a funny voice, emailing a friend to reminisce about a happy memory, watching a funny YouTube video, telling your favourite joke, doing something for someone else that makes you feel good, giving someone a genuine compliment and seeing their face light up. Choose three things to do each day. This could be the same three things each day so that it becomes a routine and habit, or you can mix it up and change each week. Try it for yourself and see how it goes! You have got nothing to lose and everything to gain!

1 thing that makes me smile	1 thing that makes me smile	1 thing that makes me smile

Thank you to everyone who has been a part of my journey. To friends and family, to school and study buddies, to work colleagues and flat mates, to travel companions and the strangers that became friends for a day. To those who have sadly passed but shared their love and knowledge with me, and to those who left my life as quickly as they arrived. For the laughs and love you have given me, for the heartache and valuable lessons I have learnt from you, and for the adventures I've been able to have along the way. Thank you for the wonderful memories and for contributing to who I am today!

Shine brightly beautiful people, the world seems big but overtime becomes small, and it is by far a better place with you in it and when you are smiling. Be true to yourself and enjoy the bumpy ride called life. Do what makes you happy and feels right for you. Because we only get one chance at life and we owe it to ourselves to live, love, and laugh always. xx

---

LIKE WHAT YOU HAVE READ?

Leave a review and follow me on Facebook and Instagram @tessasillifant I'd love to connect with you! xx

Want to view some photographs linked to this book and my travels? Find me at www.tessasillifant.com/book

Printed in Great Britain
by Amazon

52955713R00056